CLASSIC STREAMLINERS

PHOTO ARCHIVE

The Trains and the Designers

John Kelly

Iconografix
Photo Archive Series

Iconografix
PO Box 446
Hudson, Wisconsin 54016 USA

Library of Congress Control Number: 2003116192

ISBN 1-58388-114-X

04 05 06 07 08 09 5 4 3 2 1

Printed in China

Cover and book design by Dan Perry

Copyediting by Suzie Helberg

Cover photo- Illinois Central Railroad welcomed you aboard this first generation streamliner, the Green Diamond in Chicago, March 20, 1936. The five-car train was two-tone green and Pullman-built with 1200-hp Electro-Motive engines. *Pullman Company publicity photo, JM Gruber collection*

BOOK PROPOSALS

Iconografix is a publishing company specializing in books for transportation enthusiasts. We publish in a number of different areas, including Automobiles, Auto Racing, Buses, Construction Equipment, Emergency Equipment, Farming Equipment, Railroads & Trucks. The Iconografix imprint is constantly growing and expanding into new subject areas.

Authors, editors, and knowledgeable enthusiasts in the field of transportation history are invited to contact the Editorial Department at Iconografix, Inc., PO Box 446, Hudson, WI 54016.

CONTENTS

⊰ ACKNOWLEDGMENTS ⊱

This book is dedicated to my partner and best friend, Linda Marie Shult for her appreciation of railroad history and for sharing the journey. Also to the legacy of the great industrial designers: Raymond Loewy, Henry Dreyfuss, and Otto Kuhler.

My sincere thanks to industrial designer Cesar Vergara for writing the Foreword. Cesar's remarks bring together modern-day design with the streamline design era of this book.

The following friends contributed historic photographs from their collections:
JM Gruber, Paul Knutson, Bill Raia, Richard Stoving (Edward L. May collection), Jay Williams, Douglas Wornom, Grayland Station, Bob's Photos and Dr. Hans-Erhard Lessing.

Special thanks to Barbara Hall and Jon Williams of the Hagley Museum and Library for assistance on the Pennsylvania Railroad. Thyssenkrupp-Budd Company for help on the Burlington Zephyr. Henry Dreyfuss Associates-New York City. Nick Fry-Baltimore & Ohio Railroad Historical Society. Also to Dylan Frautschi, Managing Editor and the Iconografix staff for publishing this book.

I hope you enjoy the streamline era photographs selected for this book. They reflect railroads' vintage years when colorful passenger trains were styled by industrial designers and train travel was the established mode of transportation in the United States. A time when the Broadway Limited, 20th Century Limited, and Capitol Limited carried passengers in deluxe, overnight accommodations from New York City and Washington D.C. to Chicago.

John Kelly
Madison, Wisconsin
August 20, 2003

✦ FOREWORD ✦

Industrial design of passenger locomotives was a largely forgotten craft in North America for many years after the mid 1950s. The greatest challenge for a designer of our era is to create locomotives that have a definitive American flair, without harking back too strongly to the era of the great American streamlined locomotives. The danger in trying to simply "update" a look from 40 or more years ago is that it will be a diluted version of the original. One of the most peculiar things about classic industrial design, if there is such a thing, certainly holds true about Classic architecture: neither attempted to copy great ideas of others or of the past. Originality in thinking must prevail over the pull of nostalgia. For us designers, time is the hardest judge. For Loewy, Dreyfuss, Stevens and Kuhler, the judgment is favorable, as they succeeded in creating industrial and travel icons of their era. They helped define the 20th Century.

At the same time, a totally random appearance for a significant new engine is not acceptable either, though a certain air to indicate its roots does give it strength. It is in that narrow band that I operate when configuring a new American diesel–electric.

A good example is the design of Amtrak's GE Genesis. The parameters under which I worked were very different from those of the past. For one, the earlier cab was either in the middle of the engine, as in the Loewy GG-1, or in the back. The locomotives were not calculated for crash worthiness and there were no creature comforts in the cab, as we know them today. And yet, the design projects are similar, in that many times they are done under duress and without the support of the executives. One or two individuals will always push for you and allow creativity to flourish, but at great risk, because the majority of the executives and board members of a railroad will usually have a hard time understanding the value of industrial design.

I have had the good fortune of configuring both the Genesis locomotive and the Alstom EMD PL42AC. During the design process my thoughts reflected on past great American locomotives, but comparing the work of Loewy, Dreyfuss and Kuhler to my own was more inspirational than factual. The Genesis shape was the result of adherence to the clearance diagram and demand for crash worthiness. I sometimes come to think of this as aesthetic compliance. The PL42AC design work was similar, with the greatest variation being that I did not have to sell as hard. I like engines to be honest in their shape and to say, "I pull." There is something about an engine that captivates train fans and non-fans alike. Engines are way up there in the feeding chain of aesthetics. They have to look good for several generations to come.

My hope is that 30 years from now my work will not have faded into the junkyard of industrial design, but be remembered for surrounding structural engineering specifications in an attractive package with clean, bold lines.

Cesar Vergara,
Ridgefield, Connecticut
August 20, 2003.

✠ INTRODUCTION ✠

The 1930's streamline era was America's transportation age, a time when planes, trains and automobiles were given streamline styling by America's industrial designers. Glamorous trains were built from sleek stainless steel with smooth surfaces, flowing curves and bullet shapes. The trains evoked speed and modernism with names like Zephyr, Rocket, and 20th Century Limited. Almost as famous as the streamliners themselves were the industrial designers who planned them: Raymond Loewy, Henry Dreyfuss, Otto Kuhler, and the Electro-Motive Division styling team. Working independently, these young designers rose to great popularity, defining the new look for their railroad customers with smooth-shrouded locomotives and deluxe, lightweight trains. Streamlining was a by-product of the art deco movement with bright colors and curves based on aeronautical theory and function. Aircraft engineers, implying a shape that cut down on wind resistance, first used the term "streamline."

The combined effects of the 1930's Great Depression and the popularity of the automobile had caused huge declines in passenger train travel. The railroads saw streamlining as a way to bring passengers back to the trains. To many forward-looking Americans, streamlining became synonymous with progress as the country moved toward recovery and growth. The 1933 Century of Progress Exposition in Chicago helped pioneer the streamline concept. Companies showing innovative equipment at the Exposition included Pullman Car & Manufacturing Company and gas-motorcar builder Electro-Motive Corporation. Two decision-making rail-road executives attending the Exposition were clearly impressed with the new technology, E. H. Harriman (Union Pacific) and Ralph Budd (Chicago, Burlington & Quincy).

In 1934, a new era dawned for American railroads when Union Pacific and Chicago, Burlington & Quincy introduced two experimental trains, the M-10000 and Zephyr 9900. The trains were the nation's first streamliners and revolutionized American passenger train travel. With the tremendous success of the M-10000 and Zephyr 9900, the railroads turned to the industrial designers for assistance. Soon, brightly colored passenger trains, both steam and diesel-powered, were moving across America.

One of the greatest industrial designers in the 1930s was Raymond Loewy (1893-1986), a debonair, Clark Gable look-alike who was born in France. He came to New York in 1919 after serving with distinction during World War I in the French army. Loewy began his career working as a fashion designer for Vogue and Harper's Bazaar. His first railroad assignment was designing trashcans for New York's Pennsylvania Station.

In 1935, Loewy did the final restyling of the Pennsylvania Railroad GG1 double-ended, electric locomotive with bi-directional center cab. He streamlined the engine by designing a smooth locomotive body that was welded instead of riveted. The GG1 was painted dark Brunswick green, accented with gold "cat whisker" striping. Many people associated the GG1's unusual shape with the Pennsylvania Railroad, and for years the GG1 served as that railroad's symbol. Between

1934 and 1943, 139 GG1 electric locomotives were produced (57 for freight and 82 for passenger service) at a cost of $250,000 each.

After the successful GG1, Loewy designed the bullet-nosed, K4 Pacific 3768 streamline steam locomotive in 1936. Loewy's other significant railroad design was Pennsylvania's "Fleet of Modernism." The Fleet debuted June 15, 1938, and included the Broadway Limited, the General, Liberty Limited and Spirit of St. Louis. Pullman-Standard built new lightweight, all-room sleeping cars for the 1938 Broadway Limited, New York to Chicago train. They were painted Tuscan red with a darker red window panel and gold leaf pinstripes along the car's length. The Pennsylvania name stretched in bold sans serif lettering across the top letterboard of each car. The S1 6-4-4-6 locomotive, his next project, was a featured attraction at the 1939 New York World's Fair. Only one S1 was built because of the locomotive's long, rigid wheelbase. It had trouble negotiating curves in Pittsburgh, so the engine worked mostly between Chicago and Crestline, Ohio. Another Loewy trademark was the "Prow Nose" T1 4-4-4-4 locomotives of 1942, pictured on Pennsylvania Railroad timetables and magazine advertising.

In his autobiography *Never Leave Well Enough Alone*, Loewy recalled how he loved to pose beside his big engines and talked about 90 mph cab rides on the running boards.

Loewy also planned the 1939 Missouri Pacific Eagle with its striking blue and light gray scheme. The locomotive's round, side porthole windows and eagle wing emblem were distinctive. In 1947, Loewy modernized the Monon Route, combining "The Hoosier Line" slogan with the railroad's Indiana heritage. His final railroad design was for Northern Pacific's North Coast Limited in 1952. Loewy's subtle, two-tone green livery mirrored the lush shades of the train's Pacific Northwest terminus. Loewy's non-railroad design work included the Greyhound Scenicruiser Bus, the Studebaker Avanti, and Air Force One for President John F. Kennedy.

Into direct competition with the Broadway Limited steamed the train of the era, New York Central's 20th Century Limited, designed by Henry Dreyfuss (1904-1972).

The new Pullman-Standard-built train premiered June 15, 1938. From the deluxe gray-and-silver exterior colors to the stylish, informal interiors, the 20th Century Limited was a streamliner of subtle elegance. Dreyfuss's styling extended to the dining car china, silver, menus, and ashtrays—all bore the distinctive 20th Century logo of repeated horizontal bars. To pull the new train, Dreyfuss designed ten J-3a streamlined Hudson locomotives for New York-Chicago service. The Hudson's distinctive shrouding made it more powerful looking. Thundering across Ohio and Indiana with its commanding finned nose, the J-3a Hudson locomotive took passengers into the heart of streamlining.

When *Time Magazine* editors selected one industrial icon to represent the twentieth century, they chose the Dreyfuss-designed Hudson locomotive.

Dreyfuss used the term "Cleanlined" in his work, and the J-3a Hudson excelled in clean lines and functionality. New York Central was justifiably proud of his design, and the chic locomotive became the signature on advertising brochures for the "Great Steel Fleet," a slogan that became popular after the conversion from wooden passenger cars to steel cars in the early twentieth century. In addition, the designer streamlined the New York Central's 1936 Mercury passenger train. Dreyfuss came to prominence in the 1930s when he was an apprentice to flamboyant theater designer Norman Bel Geddes. By favoring practicality over art deco styling, Dreyfuss gained the respect of his blue-chip clients including Bell Telephone, Honeywell and John Deere.

German-born industrial designer Otto Kuhler (1894-1977) came to America in 1923. He worked for the Brill Company, and by 1932 was a design consultant to the American Locomotive Company (Alco). Kuhler had a talent for conveying the scale and sheer force of the steam locomotive. Commenting on his streamlined steam engine designs in his autobiography *My Iron Journey*, he wrote, "My primary objective as an artist was not to cater to the industry itself, but to reach the public. The small boy that remains in every adult is fascinated by the sights and sounds of trains, and I wanted to satisfy the longing for excitement and romance in these train-lovers." Kuhler's most famous work was arguably the Class-A 4-4-2 Atlantic streamlined steam locomotive, built by Alco for the Milwaukee Road's Hiawatha in 1935. The train's styling included brilliant bands of orange and maroon colors trimmed with gray. The locomotive was fitted with aerodynamic shrouding. Wrapped across the front of the locomotive was a huge stainless-steel wing emblem, suggesting flight and speed, and on the boiler's sides were the Hiawatha nameplates. The Hiawatha's were impressive with a distinctive shape unlike other steam locomotives.

Kuhler's other well-publicized railroad work included modernizing Baltimore & Ohio's (B&O) Royal Blue train in 1937. He also streamlined the B&O bus fleet that transferred passengers from New York City to the Jersey City terminal used by B&O passenger trains. In 1938, Kuhler updated B&O's Capitol Limited in the handsome Civil War blue-and-gray color scheme. He even streamlined the railroad's well-known Capitol Dome herald, placing a simpler, bolder rendering of the logo above a distinctive band sporting the B&O initials.

Kuhler also styled the Gulf, Mobile & Northern Rebel and did consulting work for the Lehigh Valley Railroad and the Southern Railway.

In 1937, Santa Fe Railway premiered the streamlined Super Chief by Chicago designer-decorator Sterling McDonald, who partnered with Electro-Motive Corporation (EMC) color stylist Leland Knickerbocker (1893-1939). It was McDonald who developed Santa Fe's Southwest Indian theme, and Knickerbocker who painted the classic Warbonnet red-and-silver livery, creating one of the most famous railroad images of all time. As more and more railroads converted from steam to diesel power, they turned to the EMC styling section for assistance. EMC offered this industrial design service free to its rail customers. On January 1, 1941, Winton Engine merged with Electro-Motive Corporation, forming the Electro-Motive Division (EMD) of General Motors. After the merger, assembly line locomotives were produced at the EMD plant in La Grange, Illinois, with only the paint schemes designating one railroad from another. From 1937 to 1960 it was the EMD stylists who developed the art deco paint schemes that became streamliner classics. Trackside favorites included Rock Island's red, silver and maroon, Kansas City Southern's red, yellow and green, Seaboard Air Line's citrus yellow and orange with dark green, and Illinois Central's chocolate brown and orange.

The streamline concept remained popular with the railroads, although by 1960 private automobiles, interstate highways and airlines would cut deeply into passenger rail travel. Railroad commerce soon moved toward freight-only operations, which would become their primary source of revenue. But historians have recorded the great industrial designers like Loewy, Dreyfuss and Kuhler—the men who styled the streamliners that dominated passenger rail for over 30 years.

CHAPTER ONE: *First Generation Streamliners*

Chicago Century of Progress Exposition (1933-1934) and the New York World of Tomorrow Fair (1939-1940) were important events during America's streamline, art deco era. *Author's collection*

UNION PACIFIC

Pioneers Again

TWO-THIRDS of a century has passed since Union Pacific, at the Driving of the Golden Spike, leaped into prominence as a railway pioneer. This was at Promontory, Utah, on May 10, 1869, and linked the Atlantic with the Pacific Coast by rail. Today Union Pacific is still pioneering.

"The executive officers of the Union Pacific," said W. A. Harriman, chairman of the board of directors in his official statement on May 23, 1933, "several months ago reached the conclusion that to save and restore passenger business to the rails would necessitate the development of a radically different type of passenger equipment."

Here is a completely new type of railway train, graceful in form, highly pleasing in color harmonies, and preeminent in utility, convenience and comfort.

DRIVERS CAB — 600 HORSE POWER V-TYPE MOTOR — AIR CONDITIONING & HEATING SYSTEMS — CARS HINGED TOGETHER ON ARTICULATED TRUCKS . . . CLOSED VESTIBULES — ENTRANCES WITH FOLDING STEPS — WASH ROOMS — TOTAL LENGTH OF TRAIN 204 FEET — BUFFET KITCHEN

RAILWAY POST OFFICE — BAGGAGE — PASSENGER COMPARTMENT . . . SEATING CAPACITY 60 PEOPLE — PASSENGER COMPARTMENT . . . SEATING CAPACITY 56 PEOPLE

● As a color for the exterior of the new train, canary yellow was selected after exhaustive tests. It was chosen as an additional safety measure. Canary yellow can be seen for a greater distance than any other color and its blended combination with golden brown trim constitutes one of the outstanding features of the train.

SUPER SPEED—WITH SAFETY—AND COMFORT

"Tomorrow's Train Today," 1934 Union Pacific brochure for the M-10000, the first lightweight streamliner built by the Pullman Company. *Author's collection*

Matchbook cover,
Author's collection

Union Pacific's M-10000 on
display at Pullman's south
side Chicago factory in 1934.
JM Gruber collection

11

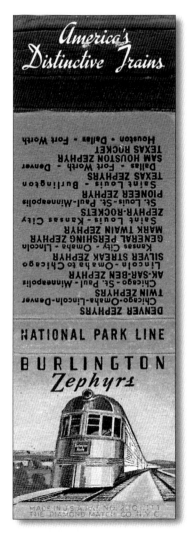

Burlington Zephyr 9900 combined the best of art deco and modern science. The train was christened Zephyr (after Zephyrus—mythical Greek God of West Wind). *Photo courtesy Thyssenkrupp-Budd Company, Philadelphia*

Aerial view of Budd Company's Philadelphia plant where beautiful train cars were made of shining stainless steel. Note the railroad sidings between the two large buildings in the upper right of the photo. *Photo courtesy Thyssenkrupp-Budd Company, Philadelphia*

Union Pacific M-10000 and Burlington Zephyr 9900 photographed at Kansas City Union Station 1934. *Electro-Motive Corporation publicity photo, Author's collection*

Aeronautical engineer William Stout designed the Pullman-built Railplane. Railplane was the prototype for Union Pacific's M-10000 and Burlington's Zephyr 9900. Photographed at Chicago in 1934. *JM Gruber collection*

In 1934, Baltimore & Ohio (B&O) had two trainsets built, one of Cor-Ten steel, the other of aluminum for service on the "Royal Blue Line" between Washington and Jersey City, New Jersey. B&O Train 28-Royal Blue accelerated past Ivy City (Washington) en route to Jersey City, New Jersey on a cold February 9, 1936, led by 4-6-4 Hudson "Lord Baltimore" locomotive 2. *Bruce Fales photo, Jay Williams collection*

The Royal Blue's sister train was reassigned to B&O subsidiary Alton Route for St. Louis-Chicago service and renamed the Ann Rutledge. B&O Class J-1 "Lady Baltimore" locomotive 1, departed St. Louis Union Station, September 17, 1937, with the Ann Rutledge for Chicago. Both "Lord and Lady Baltimore" locomotives were painted Royal Blue to match their trains. *Bruce Fales photo, Jay Williams collection*

Considered the first self-contained, box-cab diesel-electric built, Electro-Motive locomotive 50 (1800-hp) is on Baltimore & Ohio controlled Alton Route at Bloomington, Illinois, April 17, 1936. *JM Gruber collection*

Sloped-faced, box-cab diesel-electric locomotive 50 was lettered for the Abraham Lincoln (Chicago-St. Louis) train on Baltimore & Ohio subsidiary Alton Route, circa 1936. *JM Gruber collection*

Long before the streamline era, Illinois Central used a green diamond for its company logo. So a logical name for its 1936 streamliner was the Green Diamond with daily 588-mile, round-trip Chicago-St. Louis service. Train is shown departing IC Central Station at 12th Street and Michigan in downtown Chicago. *JM Gruber collection*

Aeolus (mythical Greek Keeper of the Winds), the world's first stainless steel streamlined steam locomotive proudly displayed the Burlington Route herald at La Crosse, Wisconsin in 1940. Locomotive 4000 was rebuilt from S-4 3002, at West Burlington, Iowa shops. Aeolus served as backup for the Denver Zephyrs and Twin Zephyrs. *Bill Raia collection*

Pages 22-23: In 1935-1936, Union Pacific premiered the "City" streamliners in partnership with Chicago & North Western and Southern Pacific. The primary "City" trains offered passenger service from Chicago to Portland, Los Angeles, San Francisco and Denver. Union Pacific 1938 "City" travel brochure. *Author's collection*

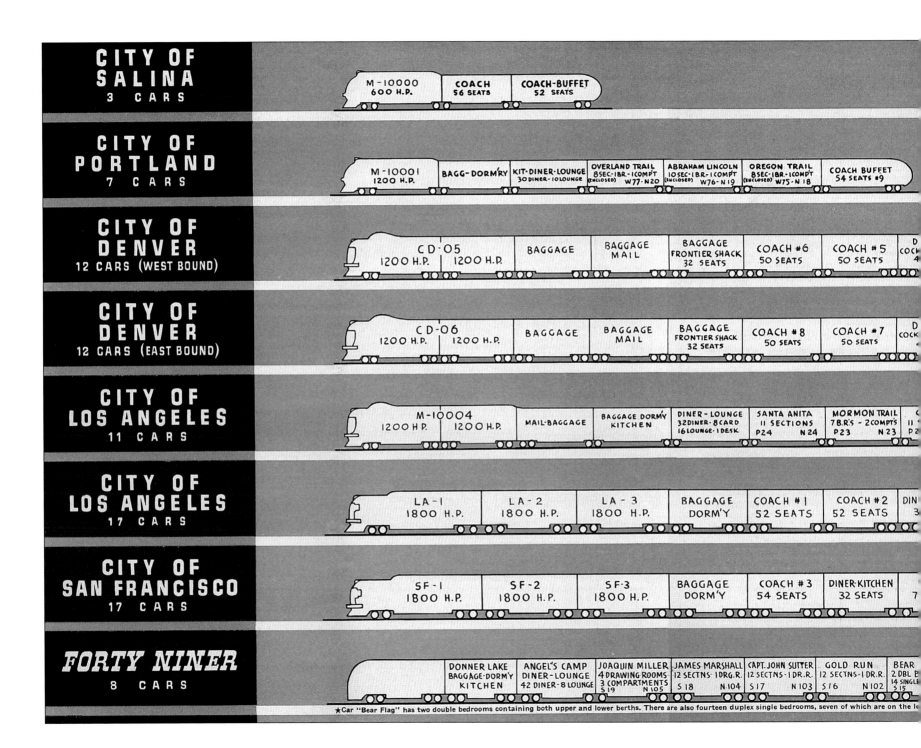

CITY OF SALINA
3 CARS

| M-10000 600 H.P. | COACH 56 SEATS | COACH-BUFFET 52 SEATS |

CITY OF PORTLAND
7 CARS

| M-10001 1200 H.P. | BAGG-DORM'RY | KIT-DINER-LOUNGE 30 DINER-10 LOUNGE | OVERLAND TRAIL 8 SEC-1 BR-1 COMP'T (ENCLOSED) W77-N20 | ABRAHAM LINCOLN 10 SEC-1 BR-1 COMP'T (ENCLOSED) W76-N19 | OREGON TRAIL 8 SEC-1 BR-1 COMP'T (ENCLOSED) W75-N18 | COACH BUFFET 54 SEATS #9 |

CITY OF DENVER
12 CARS (WEST BOUND)

| CD-05 1200 H.P. | 1200 H.P. | BAGGAGE | BAGGAGE MAIL | BAGGAGE FRONTIER SHACK 32 SEATS | COACH #6 50 SEATS | COACH #5 50 SEATS | D COCK 4 |

CITY OF DENVER
12 CARS (EAST BOUND)

| CD-06 1200 H.P. | 1200 H.P. | BAGGAGE | BAGGAGE MAIL | BAGGAGE FRONTIER SHACK 32 SEATS | COACH #8 50 SEATS | COACH #7 50 SEATS | D COCK |

CITY OF LOS ANGELES
11 CARS

| M-10004 1200 H.P. | 1200 H.P. | MAIL-BAGGAGE | BAGGAGE DORM'Y KITCHEN | DINER-LOUNGE 32 DINER-8 CARD 16 LOUNGE-1 DESK | SANTA ANITA 11 SECTIONS P24 N24 | MORMON TRAIL 7 B.R.'S-2 COMPT'S P23 N23 | 11 P2 |

CITY OF LOS ANGELES
17 CARS

| LA-1 1800 H.P. | LA-2 1800 H.P. | LA-3 1800 H.P. | BAGGAGE DORM'Y | COACH #1 52 SEATS | COACH #2 52 SEATS | DIN 3 |

CITY OF SAN FRANCISCO
17 CARS

| SF-1 1800 H.P. | SF-2 1800 H.P. | SF-3 1800 H.P. | BAGGAGE DORM'Y | COACH #3 54 SEATS | DINER-KITCHEN 32 SEATS | 7 |

FORTY NINER
8 CARS

| DONNER LAKE BAGGAGE-DORM'Y KITCHEN | ANGEL'S CAMP DINER-LOUNGE 42 DINER-8 LOUNGE | JOAQUIN MILLER 4 DRAWING ROOMS 3 COMPARTMENTS S 19 N 105 | JAMES MARSHALL 12 SECTNS-1 DRG.R. S 18 N 104 | CAPT. JOHN SUTTER 12 SECTNS-1 DR.R. S 17 N 103 | GOLD RUN 12 SECTNS-1 DR.R. S 16 N 102 | BEAR 2 DBL B 14 SINGLE S 15 |

★Car "Bear Flag" has two double bedrooms containing both upper and lower berths. There are also fourteen duplex single bedrooms, seven of which are on the le

22

The NORTH WESTERN - UNION PACIFIC
FAMOUS FLEET OF POWERFUL
Streamliners
and *THE FORTY-NINER*
PROVIDE UNEXCELLED HIGH·SPEED SERVICE
TO ALL THE WEST

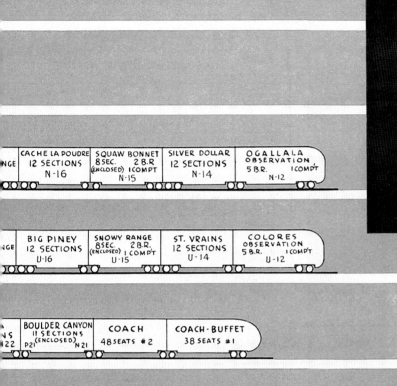

| CACHE LA POUDRE 12 SECTIONS N-16 | SQUAW BONNET 8 SEC. 2 B.R. (ENCLOSED) 1 COMPT N-15 | SILVER DOLLAR 12 SECTIONS N-14 | OGALLALA OBSERVATION 5 B.R. 1 COMPT N-12 |

| BIG PINEY 12 SECTIONS U-16 | SNOWY RANGE 8 SEC. 2 B.R. (ENCLOSED) 1 COMPT U-15 | ST. VRAINS 12 SECTIONS U-14 | COLORES OBSERVATION 5 B.R. 1 COMP'T U-12 |

| BOULDER CANYON 11 SECTIONS (ENCLOSED) P21 N 21 | COACH 48 SEATS #2 | COACH-BUFFET 38 SEATS #1 |

| DINER 72 SEATS | LITTLE-NUGGET DORM'Y-CLUB | SANTA MONICA 4 COMP'TS - 3 D.R. P-31 N-40 | WILSHIRE 12 OPEN SECTIONS N-41 | SAN DOMINGUEZ 4 COMP'TS - 3 D.R. P-32 N-42 | SAN FERNANDO 13 ROOMETTES 1 OPEN SECTION P-34 N-43 | ARROYO SECO 11 BEDROOMS P-35 N-44 | BEVERLY HILLS 12 ENC. SECTIONS P-36 N-45 | ROSE BOWL 5 BEDROOMS 12 SINGLE ROOMS P-37 N-46 | SUN VALLEY OBSERVATION-LOUNGE 36 SEATS |

| EMBARCADERO DORM'Y CLUB | TWIN PEAKS 4 COMP'TS -3 D.R. S-120 N 120 | CHINATOWN 12 OPEN SECTIONS S 121 N-121 | FISHERMAN'S WHARF 4 COMP'TS - 3 D.R. S-122 N-122 | GOLDEN GATE PARK 12 OPEN SECTIONS S-123 N-123 | SEAL ROCKS 11 BEDROOMS S-124 N-124 | UNION SQUARE 12 OPEN SECTIONS S-125 N-125 | TELEGRAPH HILL 18 ROOMETTES S-126 N-126 | PORTSMOUTH SQ. 5 BEDROOMS 12 SINGLE ROOMS S-127 N-127 | NOB HILL OBSERVATION-LOUNGE 36 SEATS |

| CALIFORNIA REPUBLIC OBSERVATION 3 BD.RMS - 1 COMP'T 514 N 100 |

seven on the upper level.

This imposing fleet of superb Streamliners . . . and the luxurious streamlined, steam-powered "Forty Niner" . . . provide unsurpassed service, fast and comfortable, to all the West.

The recently completed Streamliners, "City of Los Angeles" and "City of San Francisco," with motor units developing 5400 horsepower, are THE MOST POWERFUL DIESEL-DRIVEN TRAINS IN THE WORLD and absolutely new from "stem to stern."

The rare beauty of interior turnishings . . . the distinctive and unusual features developed for the comfort and convenience of passengers . . . make it a genuine pleasure to travel on these splendid trains.

The Streamliner "City of San Francisco" and the "Forty Niner" operate via the North Western-Union Pacific-Southern Pacific Overland Route.

Pullman Cars are shown here by name and loading number—westbound prefix being "N" in all cases. Coaches are identified by number.

RESERVATIONS FOR SPACE ON THESE TRAINS

As accommodations on these trains are limited, reservations for space, Pullman or coach, should be made as far in advance as possible.

The Streamliners and the Forty Niner are operated primarily for through passengers but will carry passengers between certain local points. Consult agent for particulars.

Reduced fare tickets for clergy, charity, etc., are not honored on these trains, except all classes of tickets are honored on "The Streamliner, City of Denver."

Union Pacific's diesel-powered City of Denver began passenger scrvice from Chicago on June 6, 1936. The train was photographed in Chicago, Illinois, led by an Electro-Motive diesel locomotive. *Earnest Mueller photo*

Union Pacific's City of Denver streamliner was ready to depart Denver Union Station in 1936. Note the Electro-Motive (General Motors) automobile style front grille on the locomotive. *JM Gruber photo*

Union Pacific's City of San Francisco began service to the Bay Area, June 14, 1936. EMD E6 985A was leading a fast City of San Francisco passenger train on a beautiful day near La Fox, Illinois. *JM Gruber collection*

Pulled by E6 locomotive LA-4, 17-car City of Los Angeles posed for the company photographer in 1941. The train initiated Chicago-Los Angeles passenger service, May 15, 1936. *Grayland Station collection*

Chicago's Dearborn Station was the scene for Santa Fe Railway's open house on February 12, 1938. Gleaming Electro-Motive E1 locomotive 3 (Super Chief) and 6 (El Capitan) surrounded the Hudson 3460 "Blue Goose," (named for the color of its shrouding). *JM Gruber collection*

CHAPTER 2: *Raymond Loewy - Pennsylvania Railroad*

Raymond Loewy posed on his S1-designed locomotive at the 1939 New York World's Fair. Loewy commented, "Nothing gave me greater pleasure I suppose than my work on the S1 locomotive for the Pennsylvania Railroad." *Hagley Museum and Library*

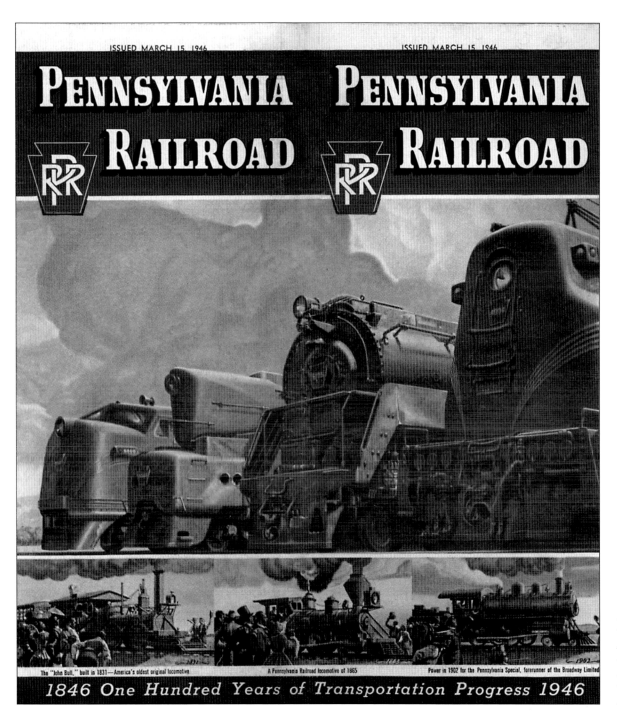

Pennsylvania Railroad 100th Anniversary passenger timetable illustrating Raymond Loewy styled locomotives. *Author's collection*

Raymond Loewy did the final styling on Pennsylvania Railroad's famous GG1 electric locomotives. Loewy's comment on the GG1 was, "Brute force can have a very sophisticated appearance, almost of great finesse and at the same time be a monster of power." *Hagley Museum and Library*

Pennsylvania Railroad exhibited the Loewy styled K4 Pacific locomotive 3768 at Washington Union Station, May 1938. The 3768 locomotive would lead the redesigned Broadway Limited, overnight all-Pullman (New York-Chicago) train of June 1938. Note the GG1 4854 electric locomotive also on display. *Bruce Fales photo, Jay Williams collection*

Another view of Pennsylvania's K4 Pacific 3768 painted dark gunmetal with gold lettering and striping, on exhibition at Washington Union Station, May 1938. Note the winged PRR keystone emblem across the locomotive's nose. *Bruce Fales photo, Jay Williams collection*

Pennsylvania Railroad locomotive 3768 (Broadway Limited) posed with Loewy-designed Studebaker automobile, photographed in Chicago 1938. *JM Gruber collection*

Pennsylvania Railroad's 1938 Broadway Limited was not completely streamlined. The train did have lightweight sleeping cars, but used a heavyweight baggage car, RPO and diner. Loewy-designed K4 Pacific locomotive 3768 shown with test train at Rockville, Pennsylvania. *Hagley Museum and Library*

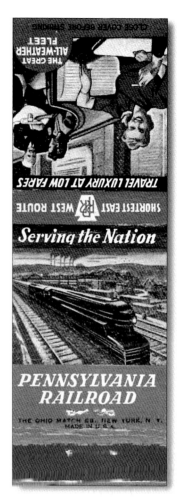

Matchbook cover,
Author's collection

Raymond Loewy designed the S1 locomotive
and Pennsylvania Railroad Altoona Shops
built the oversize steam engine in 1939.
Hagley Museum and Library

The Loewy-designed S1 locomotive 6100 served as ambassador for the railroad industry at the 1939 New York World's Fair. It was lettered "American Railroads" and displayed on a treadmill for viewing. *Jay Williams collection*

Pennsylvania Railroad's S1 6100 was leading a passenger train at Chicago. Because of the tight curves in Pittsburgh, the S1 spent most of its career hauling passenger trains between Chicago and Crestline, Ohio. *Grant Oaks photo, JM Gruber collection*

Raymond Loewy pencil drawing of the proposed S2 locomotive with cutaway view of running gear. *Hagley Museum and Library*

Matchbook cover, *Author's collection*

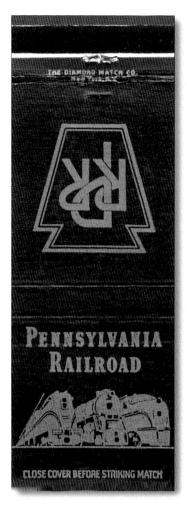

THE DIAMOND MATCH CO.
NEW YORK

PENNSYLVANIA RAILROAD

CLOSE COVER BEFORE STRIKING MATCH

Looking more like a Buck Rogers space ship than a locomotive, the T1 4-4-4-4 6110 looked fast just standing still. Louis Otto, a Raymond Loewy associate, did most of the T1 styling. *Hagley Museum and Library*

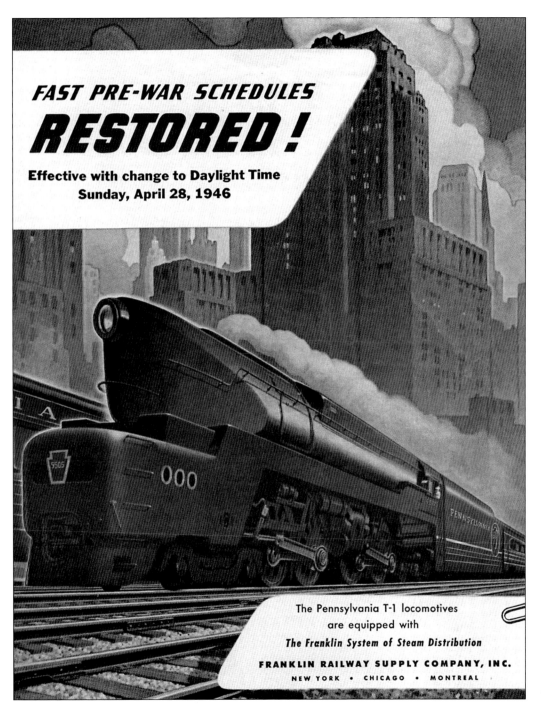

Franklin Railway Supply Company, 1946
advertisement for Pennsylvania Railroad
T1 locomotives. *Author's collection*

Pennsylvania Railroad had 52 of the "Prow Nose" T1 locomotives built and they routinely hauled passenger trains at 100 mph across the flatlands of Illinois, Indiana and Ohio. *Gene Gentsch photo, date and location unknown*

Pennsylvania Railroad's 1941 Fleet of Modernism train brochure. *Author's collection*

One of the trains in Pennsylvania Railroad's Fleet of Modernism was the Spirit of St. Louis. 4-6-2 Pacific locomotive 5492 is shown leading the New York-St. Louis passenger train at East St. Louis, Illinois, February 10, 1940. *JM Gruber collection*

PENNSYLVANIA RAILROAD *Presents* THE

TRAIL BLAZER

NEVER BEFORE on the speed lanes between New York and Chicago a train like this! It cuts through old travel ideas to bring you luxuries and comforts undreamed of in coach travel . . . yet you pay no more than for regular coach transportation. Without a doubt . . . *the greatest luxury ride for the least money!*

Pennsylvania Railroad

SHORTEST, SMOOTHEST, QUICKEST ROUTE BETWEEN EAST AND WEST

Introduced in 1939, Pennsylvania Railroad's Trail Blazer, all-coach streamliner offered service between New York and Chicago. *Author's collection*

Pullman-built, sleeper-buffet-observation car Mountain View. The car entered service in January 1949 on Pennsylvania Railroad's Broadway Limited (New York-Chicago) passenger train. *Owen Leander photo, JM Gruber collection*

Broadway Limited observation car Mountain View was ready to depart Chicago Union Station, circa 1961. *Dan Hale photo, Jay Williams collection*

Most of the GG1s were painted Brunswick green while only a few were painted Tuscan red. In July 1967, GG1 4907 pulled a heavyweight baggage car and passenger train at Linden, New Jersey. *JM Gruber collection*

The Raymond Loewy-styled GG1 electric locomotives symbolized the Pennsylvania Railroad with speed, power and elegance. GG1 4915 led a passenger train at Trenton, New Jersey in December 1965. *JM Gruber collection*

Beginning an American tradition in 1936 through 1975 (except for the war years of 1942-1944), the Pennsylvania Railroad ran annual Army-Navy football game trains from New York City and Washington DC to Philadelphia Municipal Stadium. Army-Navy Day was mostly an all GG1 locomotive operation with trains pulling coaches into Greenwich Yard in Philadelphia near the stadium. Photo circa 1950s. *JM Gruber collection*

The Baldwin-built "passenger sharknose" diesel was another Raymond Loewy inspiration. The railroad purchased 18 A-units and 9 B-units in 1948 for mainline passenger service. However, they were downgraded to secondary passenger service in favor of EMD E-units. Baldwin 5783 was photographed at Williamsport, Pennsylvania. *JM Gruber collection*

Double headlights were a rarity on Pennsylvania's Baldwin diesels. Only two A-units had them, 5770 and 5771. On July 7, 1960, locomotive 5771 crossed Morgan Drawbridge in New Jersey. *JM Gruber collection*

The Electro-Motive E7 was the locomotive that finally convinced the Pennsylvania Railroad to dieselize. E7 5874 passed the classic Williamsport, Pennsylvania depot on May 31, 1965. *JM Gruber collection*

Industrial designer Raymond Loewy's distinctive style extended to Missouri Pacific's "Route of the Eagles." Missouri Pacific E3 7000 was in charge of a nicely matched consist in blue and light gray with yellow stripes. *JM Gruber collection*

Northern Pacific's North Coast Limited-Vista-Dome car 558 (owned by CB&Q) wore the Loewy-designed two-tone green livery at Chicago, May 24, 1969. *Jay Williams collection*

The scenery is magnificent when you're flying along at

14 feet.

You're two stories high in a bubble-top railroad car aboard Northern Pacific's Vista-Dome North Coast Limited. From here, you get a magnificent close-up view of the beautiful Northwest.

You'll also enjoy good accommodations, good food and good service anytime you travel the route of the Vista-Dome North Coast Limited. This is the way to run a railroad. This is the way we run the Northern Pacific.

Reclining chair coaches
Slumbercoaches · Pullmans
Stewardess service
Chicago · Twin Cities · Billings
Spokane · Portland · Seattle

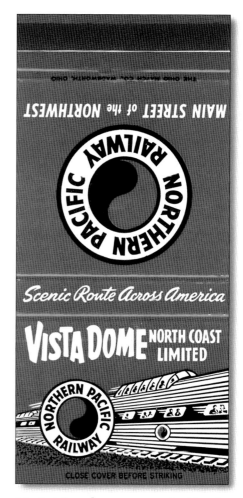

Matchbook cover, *Author's collection*

Northern Pacific Railway advertisement, circa 1960. *Author's collection*

The Monon Route's "Hoosier Line" slogan and new passenger F3's in crimson, gray and white honored the school colors of Indiana University, and were planned by Raymond Loewy in 1947. *JM Gruber collection*

CHAPTER 3: *Henry Dreyfuss - New York Central Railroad*

Henry Dreyfuss quoted, "If people are made safer, more comfortable, more eager to purchase, or just plain happier…the designer has succeeded." Photograph of Mr. Dreyfuss, circa 1965. *Photo courtesy Henry Dreyfuss Associates, New York City*

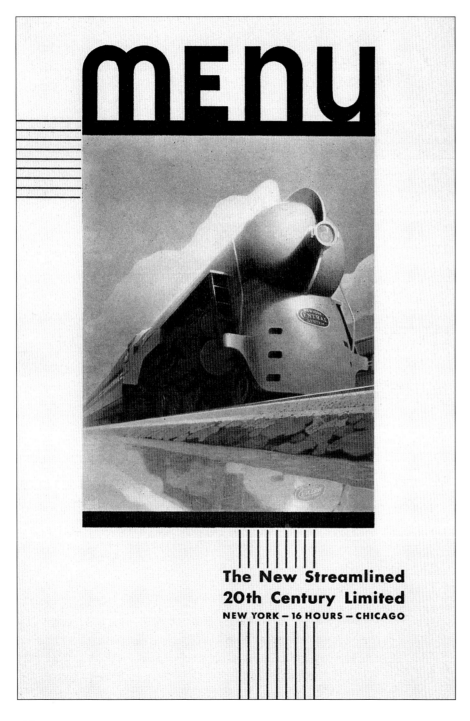

MENU

The New Streamlined
20th Century Limited
NEW YORK — 16 HOURS — CHICAGO

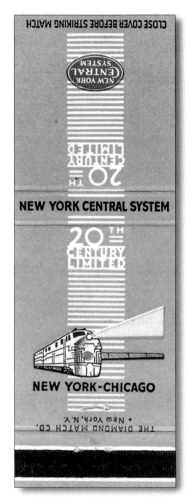

New York Central 1939 dining car menu featured the famous promotional poster of the 20th Century Limited by artist Leslie Ragan. Mr. Ragan also painted calendars for the New York Central from 1942 into the Postwar Era. *Author's collection*

New York Central's flagship 20th Century Limited, billed as "The Greatest Train in the World" at Chicago's La Salle Street Station in 1938. Note the landmark Chicago Board of Trade building in the background. *Bill Raia collection*

New York Central's 20th Century Limited captured the streamline aura past Bear Mountain Bridge along the beautiful Hudson River at Manitou, New York in 1938. *Frank Quin photo, Jay Williams collection*

"Cleanlining" was the term Henry Dreyfuss gave to his design concept. The 20th Century Limited looked very clean-of-line wearing the gray-and-silver Dreyfuss livery at Peekskill, New York, August 1, 1941. *Edward L. May memorial collection*

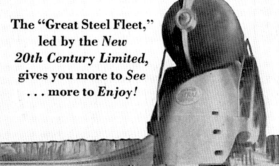

One of the most distinctive images, often compared to a Spartan warrior's helmet, was the Dreyfuss design for ten streamline J-3a Hudson locomotives. The chic locomotives fronted the 20th Century Limited and were featured in newspaper and magazine advertisements. New York Central promoted the train with 1939 era "Great Steel Fleet" brochures. *Author's collection*

Thundering by Oscawana in upstate New York, the 20th Century Limited with J-3a Hudson 5451 was making good time on August 8, 1940. *Edward L. May memorial collection*

American Locomotive Company built 50 J-3a Hudson locomotives for New York Central. The last ten locomotives were numbered 5445-5454 and streamlined by Henry Dreyfuss for the 20th Century Limited. Locomotive 5450 photographed at Englewood, Illinois, May 6, 1939. *Jay Williams collection*

"The Commodore Vanderbilt"

How the Commodore Vanderbilt appears from the front. The drop coupler is concealed behind a door at the bottom. A sturdy cowcatcher is also hidden beneath the metal front. At the top, behind the grill may be seen the tip of the smokestack.

B1619—100M—12-19-54

... World's First Streamlined High Powered Steam Locomotive

NEW YORK CENTRAL LINES

New York Central Commodore Vanderbilt 1934 train brochure. *Author's collection*

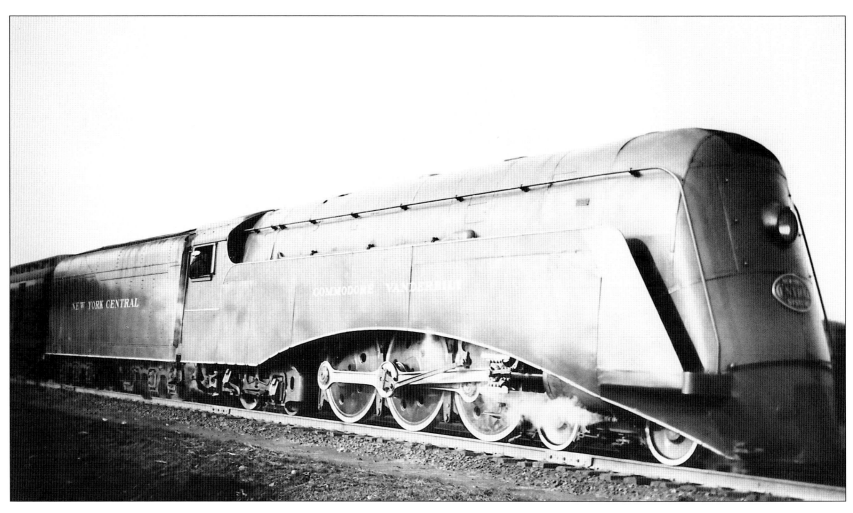

Named for the New York Central's founder, Commodore Vanderbilt, the J-1e 4-6-4 Hudson was America's first fully streamlined steam locomotive. New York Central used the locomotive to lead the heavyweight 20th Century Limited, photographed at Englewood, Illinois in 1934. *Jay Williams collection*

The engineer aboard New York Central's J-3a Hudson posed for the photographer at Chicago's La Salle Street Station with the Commodore Vanderbilt (New York-Chicago) passenger train, circa 1940. *Bill Raia collection*

J-3a Hudson locomotive 5429 posed at Harmon, New York, August 10, 1946. Note the cast-metal New York Central oval medallion and train name, Empire State Express, in script above the pilot. The Empire State Express offered daily service from Detroit, Cleveland and Buffalo to New York City. *Bill Raia collection*

New York Central chose the name Mercury to convey speed and modernism for its Cleveland-Detroit passenger train in 1936. Dreyfuss designed the Mercury, led by rebuilt K-5a Pacific 4917, and photographed near Sandusky, Ohio, July 1938. The K-5a drivers were painted aluminum and black adding to the train's aura. *Bob's Photos*

NEW YORK CENTRAL SYSTEM

TIME TABLES

New York Central
Michigan Central
Big Four Route
Pittsburgh & Lake Erie
Boston & Albany

Niagara from Falls View

The Water Level Route ~~ *You Can Sleep*

EFFECTIVE SEPTEMBER 25, 1938, FORM 101

NEW YORK CENTRAL SYSTEM

TIME TABLES

New York Central
Michigan Central
Big Four Route
Pittsburgh & Lake Erie
Boston & Albany

Grand Central Terminal, New York City

The Water Level Route ~~ *You Can Sleep*

EFFECTIVE SEPTEMBER 25, 1938, FORM 101

The "Water Level Route" slogan and "You Can Sleep" tag line were the inspiration of St. Louis advertising man Harry Lesan. New York Central 1938 passenger timetable. *Author's collection*

New York Central Train 41-Knickerbocker (New York-St. Louis) shown between Harmon and Albany, New York, along the east bank of the Hudson River, April 13, 1947. *JM Gruber collection*

Electro-Motive E7 diesels began replacing NYC streamlined Hudsons in 1945. On August 14, 1948, a pair of EMD E7s led a New York Central streamline passenger train at Poughkeepsie, New York. *John Krause photo, JM Gruber collection*

Cars purchased for re-equipping the 20th Century Limited in 1948 included sleeper-lounge-observation car Hickory Creek shown on press run at Garrison, New York, September 9, 1948. *JM Gruber collection*

All New York Central passenger trains had electric locomotives between Harmon, New York and Grand Central Terminal in New York City. Electric Class P2 225 locomotive is shown leading westbound Ohio State Limited near Spuyten Duyvil, the name 17th century Dutch settlers gave the waterway separating the northern tip of Manhattan from the Bronx. *Jay Williams collection*

New York Central locomotive E7A 4002 with initial lightning stripe paint scheme, also the work of industrial designer Henry Dreyfuss, photographed at Chicago's 63rd Street yard, January 5, 1956. *JM Gruber collection*

CHAPTER 4: *Otto Kuhler – Milwaukee Road and Baltimore & Ohio Railroad*

Otto Kuhler commented on streamstyled steam, "I realized that this was to be a revolution I would provide, sweeping away all the useless old ornamentation in favor of clean, sleek lines." Photograph of Mr. Kuhler at Chicago, Illinois, circa 1935. *Photo courtesy Dr. Hans-Erhard Lessing*

Otto Kuhler-designed and Alco-built 4-4-2 Atlantic 2, presented a powerful image departing Chicago with the 1936 Hiawatha (Chicago-Twin Cities) passenger train. *JM Gruber collection*

The Hiawatha was America's first non-articulated passenger train pulled by steam locomotives. 4-4-2 Atlantic 3 with Hiawatha in tow had a "proceed" signal from the semaphore at St. Paul, Minnesota. *JM Gruber collection*

Milwaukee Road Shops with design assistance from Otto Kuhler handcrafted the Beaver Tail observation car with welded fins, suggesting terrific speed. The car became a Milwaukee Road icon. *Midwest Hiawatha brochure, Author's collection*

Otto Kuhler told Milwaukee Road officials, "Through the use of color and line, it is possible to exude an impression of speed while standing still." Milwaukee Road previewed the new 4-6-4 Hudson F7 at Chicago Union Station in 1938. *JM Gruber collection*

Milwaukee Road Train 102-eastbound Hiawatha was led by Alco 4-6-4 Hudson F7, at St. Paul, Minnesota. A silver nameplate was mounted on the cylinder shrouding below the builder's plate that read, "Speedlined by Otto Kuhler." *Jay Williams collection*

Otto Kuhler's final and personal favorite steam "Speedlined" design was in 1940 for Southern Railway's Ps-4 locomotive 1380. The elegant green-and-silver steam engine pulled the Washington to Monroe, Virginia segment of the Tennessean. *Bob's Photos*

Gulf, Mobile & Ohio DL-109 271 at East St. Louis, Illinois, fronted the Rebel (St. Louis-New Orleans) passenger train. The Rebel wore the flashy silver-and-red scheme for predecessor Gulf, Mobile & Northern, styled by well-known designer Otto Kuhler. *JM Gruber collection*

Otto Kuhler streamlined Baltimore & Ohio's (B&O) bus fleet in 1936. The buses were painted blue-black-gold. Kuhler's newly designed B&O Capitol Dome logo was on the bus's V-shaped front end. B&O 1938 New York City map. *Author's collection*

In 1927, Baltimore & Ohio ordered 20 Baldwin-built 4-6-2 Pacific steam engines, each named after U.S. Presidents. In 1937, Otto Kuhler styled the new Royal Blue (Washington-Jersey City) passenger train for the Baltimore & Ohio. Leading the Royal Blue at Plainfield, New Jersey was Pacific engine 5304 with Kuhler trademark bullet nose and centered headlight. *Phil Buchert photo, Jay Williams collection*

In 1947, Baltimore & Ohio's first female research engineer, Olive W. Dennis, redesigned and streamlined four 20-year-old Baldwin Pacifics (5301-5304) for service on the new Cincinnatian (Washington-Cincinnati) passenger trains. Locomotive 5302 photographed at Grafton, West Virginia, circa 1950. *Bruce Fales photo, Jay Williams collection*

EA 53 with 1800-hp was one of six diesel locomotives built by Electro-Motive Corporation in 1937 for the Baltimore & Ohio Railroad. *JM Gruber collection*

Baltimore & Ohio EA 53 and EB (booster) led the Royal Blue passenger train at Plainfield, New Jersey in 1939. *Paul Buchert photo, Jay Williams collection*

Baltimore & Ohio EA 53 and EB (booster) led Train 4-Diplomat through Linden, Maryland, March 29, 1944. *Bruce Fales photo, Jay Williams collection*

Aerial view of Harpers Ferry, West Virginia, shows the confluence of the Potomac and Shenandoah Rivers below Baltimore & Ohio trackage. *Photo courtesy B&O Railroad Historical Society, circa 1928*

Baltimore & Ohio Train 6-Capitol Limited (Chicago-Washington) passenger train paused at Harpers Ferry, West Virginia, April 28, 1951. Note the B&O emblems and tail sign behind the sleeper-buffet-lounge-observation car Metcalf. *Bruce Fales photo, Jay Williams collection*

Baltimore & Ohio passenger train led by E6 58 arrived at Elizabeth, New Jersey in June 1949. *JM Gruber collection*

Baltimore & Ohio passenger train led by locomotive E8 1450 meets New York Central freight with Alco locomotive. Date and location unknown. *JM Gruber collection*

Baltimore & Ohio locomotive EA 51 and heavyweight National Limited departed the massive train shed at St. Louis Union Station. *JM Gruber collection*

Baltimore & Ohio operated some of the earliest streamline diesels in the nation. EA 54 is shown with a matched set of eight lightweight cars on the Chicago & Alton route. *JM Gruber collection*

Baltimore & Ohio passenger trains arriving in Chicago used Grand Central Station. The station opened in 1893 and closed in 1969. Remaining B&O trains transferred to Chicago & North Western Station until discontinued by Amtrak in 1971. *Photo courtesy B&O Railroad Historical Society*

Baltimore & Ohio passenger train departing Chicago & North Western Station with sleeper-buffet-lounge-observation car Wawasee in the train's mid-section, April 1971. *Doug Wornom photo*

A thrill by day...an even greater thrill by night!

THE STRATA-DOME

EXCLUSIVE B & O FEATURE BETWEEN

CHICAGO • PITTSBURGH • AKRON • WASHINGTON

It's the most exciting feature in rail travel—a glass dome floating high over the rails and offering views in every direction plus a direct view of the sky overhead.

AND AT NIGHT—FLOODLIGHTS

When the dark hours come, the powerful lights on the Strata-Dome cars are switched on, and the landscape is revealed in glowing beauty. It's a rare treat—and you can ride in the Strata-Dome at no extra charge. Try it—and relax as you ride!

STRATA-DOMES ARE ON THESE B&O DIESEL-ELECTRIC TRAINS

The Capitol Limited

All-Pullman Streamliner   Air-Conditioned
All types of sleeping accommodations
Train Secretary

The Columbian

Deluxe Coach Streamliner   Air-Conditioned
Reclining coach seats reserved
in advance without extra charge
Stewardess Service

The Shenandoah

Pullman and Coach   Air-Conditioned
All types of sleeping accommodations
Reclining coach seats   Stewardess Service

*Strata-Domes operated on the Shenandoah. Westbound from Washington on odd dates except the 31st. Eastbound from Chicago on even dates.

Through service on these trains to and from Baltimore, Philadelphia, New York

BALTIMORE & OHIO RAILROAD

No travel comfort equals train travel comfort

LINKING 13 GREAT STATES WITH THE NATION

Baltimore & Ohio advertisement for the Strata Dome car circa 1955. *Author's collection*

Baltimore & Ohio Strata Dome-Coach 5550 was built by Pullman in 1949. Note the floodlights atop the car for night viewing. Photographed at Chicago, September 21, 1968. *JM Gruber collection*

Baltimore & Ohio Electro-Motive F3s were added to the diesel roster in 1948. F3 83 photographed in the Detroit area, May 27, 1948. *JM Gruber collection*

The Chesapeake and Ohio (C&O) Railway was majority stockholder of the Baltimore & Ohio (B&O) Railroad and applied to the ICC for legal control of the B&O in January 1962. On February 4, 1963, Chesapeake and Ohio officially took control of the B&O, but each railroad retained separate identities. C&O locomotives 146 and 147 photographed at Fort Street Station in Detroit, April 1971. *Doug Wornom photo*

Electro-Motive advertisement featured New York Central's "Great Steel Fleet" circa 1949. *Author's collection*

In May 1947, General Motors subsidiary Electro-Motive Division, together with the Pullman Company, built the four-dome "Train of Tomorrow," which toured the U.S. to sell other railroads on dome cars. April 1948, Colorado Springs, Colorado. *JM Gruber collection*

Pullman-Standard built the Xplorer train for the New York Central Railroad. The Cleveland-Columbus-Cincinnati passenger train was powered by hydraulic-transmission German-built diesels, prone to frequent breakdowns. *Photo circa 1957, Bill Raia collection*

Officially labeled LWT12 (lightweight 1200-hp), Locomotive 2 was built by General Motors in 1955 to power its Aerotrain. In 1957, the locomotive and cars were sold to the Rock Island Railroad for Chicago commuter service. Today the locomotive is displayed at the National Railroad Museum-Green Bay, Wisconsin. *Author's photo*

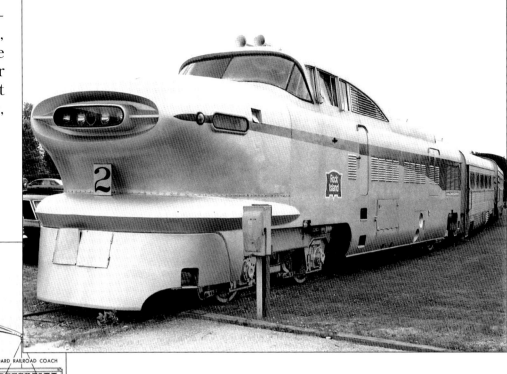

One of the famous postwar experimental trains was the General Motors Aerotrain. The futuristic locomotive had the look and feel of Detroit's automobile styles. *Electro-Motive Division brochure, Author's collection*

The Rock Island Line was a "mighty fine line," a fabled carrier of song and legend. Rock Island owned the only six TAs (Nos. 601-606) built by Electro-Motive for service on Rock Island passenger trains. EMC color stylist Leland Knickerbocker developed the red, maroon and silver colors in 1936. Rock Island TA 601 is shown leading the Peoria Rocket in 1938. *JM Gruber collection*

Rock Island parlor-observation car Peoria on the Peoria Rocket in 1938. *JM Gruber collection*

Rock Island and the Burlington Route operated joint passenger train service from Minneapolis to St. Louis, Missouri with the Zephyr-Rocket. The Zephyr-Rocket was photographed departing St. Louis Union Station, led by E3 627. *JM Gruber collection*

The Rocky Mountain Rocket (Chicago-Denver-Colorado Springs) featured streamline coaches and diners built by the Budd Company with Pullman sleeping cars. Photographed at Englewood Station near Chicago in 1946. *Grayland Station collection*

Artist drawing of Santa Fe Super Chief by Leland Knickerbocker, General Motors Art and Colour-Industrial Design Dept., April 1937. *JM Gruber collection*

Santa Fe 11, Electro-Motive E3 paused at Galesburg, Illinois as mail was loaded aboard the Chief. Note the engine crew waited patiently for the "All-aboard" call, circa 1955. *JM Gruber collection*

Santa Fe DL-109 and booster unit DL-110 were numbered 50 and 50A. Photographed at Los Angeles Union Passenger Terminal. *JM Gruber collection*

along your way

Facts about stations and scenes on the Santa Fe

Santa Fe "Along Your Way" 1953 travel brochure. *Author's collection*

After World War II, Santa Fe purchased the elegant PA-series diesels from American Locomotive Company. PA 58 with its long nose and Warbonnet red-and-silver colors added to the streamline aura. Note locomotive 58 is shown with flags to denote following sections. *JM Gruber collection*

Baggage was being loaded aboard Santa Fe's San Francisco Chief and the train was about to depart Chicago's Dearborn Station for the "Golden Gate" city, April 1971. *Doug Wornom photo*

Santa Fe's Budd-built, Hi-Level cars allowed passengers to ride in the upper level with a smooth ride and great views. Owen Leander photo, Chicago, May 30, 1969. *JM Gruber collection*

The last westbound run of the Chief took place May 13, 1968, from Chicago's Dearborn Station to Los Angeles' Union Station. Note the railfans on hand to record the historic event. *JM Gruber collection*

It's June 1971, and Amtrak is one month old, but the Chicago-Los Angeles Super Chief looked almost the same as it did under Santa Fe Railway auspices. A Fairbanks-Morse H-12-44 shoved the streamliner from the coach yard to the departure platform at Chicago's Union Station. Note the Sears Tower under construction in the background. *Doug Wornom photo*

TWO *GREAT* **TRAINS**

Between Chicago and Seattle-Portland

GREAT NORTHERN'S
Streamlined
EMPIRE BUILDER

This superb new train speeds across the top of the nation, making the 2,211-mile transcontinental journey in just two nights —45 hours of safe, smooth riding. Travel in a DUPLEX-ROOMETTE, single occupancy accommodation that costs just $2.13 more than a standard Pullman lower berth from Chicago to Seattle-Portland.

DIESEL-POWERED
Oriental Limited
GREAT NORTHERN'S VACATION TRAIN

Famous for air-conditioned comfort, the ORIENTAL LIMITED takes you to the glorious scenery of Montana's Glacier National Park and the superbly scenic Pacific Northwest. Stops daily at eastern and western entrances to Glacier Park. Great for riding, great for sleeping, great for meals.

For further information write to
V. J. Kenny, P. T. M. St. Paul 1, Minn.

Chicago Railroad
FAIR

GN

July 20 Through Labor Day 1948

Burlington Route

GREAT NORTHERN RAILWAY

SPOKANE PORTLAND AND SEATTLE RY.

This Great Northern Railway travel brochure for the 1948 Chicago Railroad Fair featured "Rocky the Goat" logo and two Great trains between Chicago and Seattle-Portland on the streamlined Empire Builder and diesel-powered Oriental Limited. *Author's Collection*

Great Northern's Empire Builder was detouring over Northern Pacific rails at Missoula, Montana in 1948 due to flood conditions. *Author's collection*

Great Northern observation-lounge cars wore Omaha orange and Pullman green with gold striping. The colors were developed by the Electro-Motive design team's locomotive styling section. Many considered it one of the finest passenger train schemes ever. *Author's collection*

New! This season ... *effective December 15th.*

DIESEL-ELECTRIC LOCOMOTIVES

ORANGE BLOSSOM SPECIAL - (EAST COAST)
First Trips—Southbound Dec. 15th; Northbound Dec. 17th

8:30 AM	Lv Boston (South Sta.)..............NYNH&H Lv		8:45 PM
9:30 AM	Lv Providence....................... " Ar		7:45 PM
11:48 AM	Lv New Haven....................... " Ar		5:27 PM
5:35 PM	Ar Washington....................... PRR Lv		11 35 AM
1:20 PM	Lv New York (Penn. Sta.)...............PRR Ar		3:30 PM
1:35 PM	Lv Newark .... " Ar		3:14 PM
2:51 PM	Lv North Philadelphia................ " Ar		1:59 PM
3:00 PM	Lv Philadelphia (30th St. Sta.)........ " Ar		1:50 PM
4:33 PM	Lv Baltimore........................ " Ar		12:15 PM
5:55 PM	Lv Washington......................RF&P Ar		11:10 AM
▼ 8:35 PM	Lv Richmond (Main St. Sta.)......SEABOARD Ar	▼ 8:28 AM
A▼ 9:05 PM	Lv Petersburg........................ " Ar	A▼ 7:57 AM
A⑯ 7:23 AM	Lv Thalmann (Brunswick-Sea Island)... " Ar	A⑯ 9:12 PM
A⑯ 8:40 AM	Ar Baldwin.......................... " Lv	A⑯ 8:05 PM
A⑯11:36 AM	Ar Winter Haven (Florence Villa)...... " Lv	A⑥ 5:04 PM
A⑥11:45 AM	Ar West Lake Wales-Lake Wales........ " Lv	A⑥ 4:54 PM
A⑯12:06 PM	Ar Avon Park........................ " Lv	A⑥ 4:32 PM
A⑯12:17 PM	Ar Sebring (Lake Jackson)............. " Lv	A⑤ 4:22 PM
A 1:52 PM	Ar West Palm Beach-Palm Beach....... " Lv	A 2:46 PM
A⑯ 2:02 PM	Ar Lake Worth........................ " Lv	A⑥ 2:36 PM
A⑯ 2:15 PM	Ar Delray Beach..................... " Lv	A⑥ 2:24 PM
A⑯ 2:30 PM	Ar Deerfield (Boca Raton)............. " Lv	A⑥ 2:24 PM
A⑯ 2:51 PM	Ar Fort Lauderdale................... " Lv	A⑤ 1:52 PM
A⑯ 3:01 PM	Ar Hollywood........................ " Lv	A⑥ 1:41 PM
3:35 PM	Ar Miami............................ " Lv	1:10 PM
7:00 PM	Lv Miami..........P&OSS For sailing dates Ar	8:00 PM
9:00 AM	Ar Havana............. Consult Ticket Agents Lv	7:00 PM
5:00 PM	Lv Miami.................. Fla. Motor Lines Ar	11:30 AM
9:30 PM	Ar Key West..................... " " Lv	7:00 AM

ORANGE BLOSSOM SPECIAL - (WEST COAST)
First Trips—Southbound Dec. 15th; Northbound Dec. 17th

8:30 AM	Lv Boston...........................NYNH&H Ar		8:45 PM
9:30 AM	Lv Providence....................... " Ar		7:45 PM
11:48 AM	Lv New Haven....................... " Ar		5:26 PM
5:35 PM	Lv Washington...................... PRR Ar		11:35 AM
1:30 PM	Lv New York (Penn. Sta.)...............PRR Ar		3:00 PM
1:40 PM	Lv Newark.......................... " Ar		2:43 PM
2:58 PM	Lv North Philadelphia................ " Ar		1:31 PM
3:07 PM	Lv Philadelphia (30th St. Sta.)........ " Ar		1:22 PM
4:37 PM	Lv Baltimore........................ " Ar		11:43 AM
6:10 PM	Lv Washington......................RF&P Ar		10:35 AM
Ar 8:51 PM	Lv Richmond (Main St. Sta.)......SEABOARD Ar	Ar 7:53 AM
Ar 9:20 PM	Lv Petersburg........................ " Ar	Ar 7:14 AM
6:42 AM	Ar Savannah (Union Sta.)............. " Lv	9:33 PM
A⑯ 7:56 AM	Ar Thalmann (Brunswick-Sea Island)... " Lv	A⑯ 8:10 PM
9:15 AM	Ar Jacksonville...................... " Lv	6:55 PM
A⑯10 57 AM	Ar Ocala (Silver Springs)............. " Lv	A⑯ 5:06 PM
A⑯12:38 PM	Ar Plant City....................... " Lv	A⑭ 3:23 PM
1:15 PM	Ar Tampa........................... " Lv	2:55 PM
A 2:18 PM	Ar Clearwater....................... " Lv	A 1:55 PM
A 2:24 PM	Ar Belleair (Belleview-Biltmore Hotel).... " Lv	A 1:49 PM
3:00 PM	Ar St Petersburg..................... " Lv	1:15 PM
3:13 PM	Ar Palmetto-Ellenton...............SEABOARD Lv	1:09 PM
3:17 PM	Ar Bradenton-Manatee................ " Lv	1:05 PM
3:35 PM	Ar Sarasota......................... " Lv	12:50 PM
4:20 PM	Ar Venice........................... " Lv	12:10 PM
4:00 PM	Ar Boca Grande.....(First trips: Sthbd. Jan. 17 " Lv	11:45 AM
4:10 PM	Ar South Boca Grande (Nthbd. Jan. 18) " Lv	11:40 AM
4:55 PM	Ar Useppa Island...................Yacht Lv	10:00 AM

Explanation of Characters shown on Pages 33-34 — Equipment on Pages 17-18.

Seaboard Railway 1939 timetable for the Orange Blossom Special. *Author's collection*

119

Seaboard Air Lines slant-nosed, Electro-Motive E4 3013 shown at Richmond, Virginia. The diesels were painted bright citrus yellow-and-orange with dark green, developed by the Electro-Motive styling group. *JM Gruber collection*

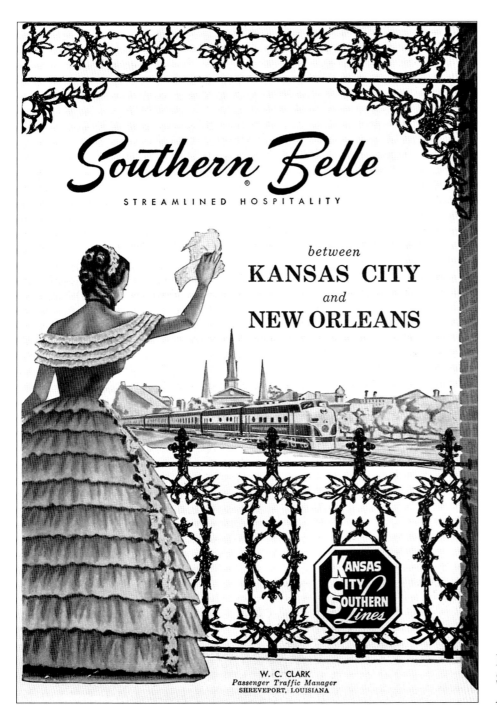

Kansas City Southern advertisement for the Southern Bell passenger train, circa April 1953. *Author's collection*

In a nostalgic view, Electro-Motive E3 21 led a Kansas City Southern heavyweight train. Date and location unknown. *JM Gruber collection*

Illinois Central's famous City of Miami, Electro-Motive E6 4000 wore the citrus orange with a green "bow wave" rising from the locomotive nose and cresting at the cab windows. The colors were later revised to the popular chocolate brown and orange. *Photograph circa 1940, JM Gruber collection*

Illinois Central's locomotive 4028, cloaked in chocolate brown and orange paint scheme, departed Chicago with a nice looking passenger train, most likely the Panama Limited. *Doug Wornom photo*

Illinois Central passenger train led by locomotive 4024 was ready to depart Chicago's Central Station. Note the Illinois Central rooftop illuminated sign. *Doug Wornom photo*

The train board in Chicago's Central Station as it looked March 6, 1972, the last day of Amtrak service at the historic station. *Doug Wornom photo*

RAILWAYS

BUSES

AMERICAN CULTURE

RECREATIONAL VEHICLES

TRUCKS

TRACTORS & CONSTRUCTION EQUIPMENT

AUTOMOTIVE

More Great Titles From Iconografix

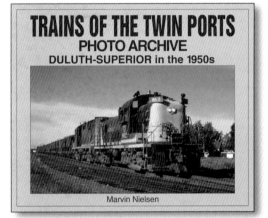
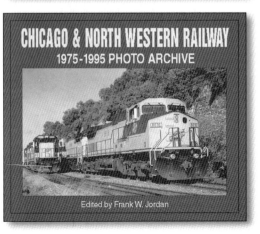

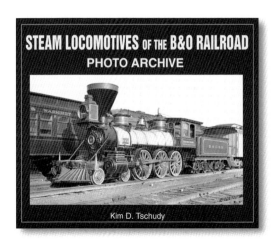
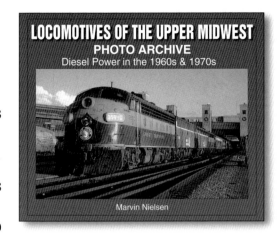
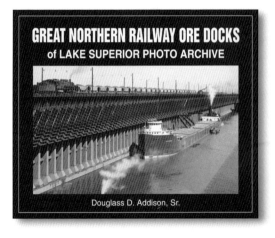
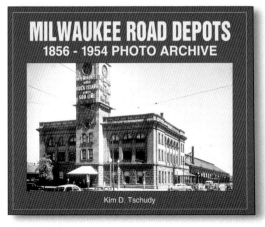